Each Week

By Cameron Macintosh

All these kids do fun things each week.

Shall we see
what they can do?

Each week,
Sam eats a meal
with Gran and Grandad.

Sam gives Grandad a kiss
on the cheek!

Tiff helps Dad each week.

They pick green peas
and dig up yams.

They pull out weeds.

Nelly is just a baby.

Each week,
Sol reads to her.

He helps Nelly get to sleep.

Lee runs with her team each week.

They run laps of the track and leap each beam.

Each week,
Keith trains at the beach.

He wants to save lives
and be chief of the beach!

Neil tends to lost pets each week.

He feeds and walks them.

Reed likes to go to speech club
each week.
He gives speeches on things
that he loves.

This week,
Reed gives a speech
on the time he rode a donkey!

These kids are lucky
to do fun things each week.

What could you do?

CHECKING FOR MEANING

1. What does Tiff help Dad with each week? *(Literal)*
2. Who helps Nelly get to sleep? *(Literal)*
3. What do you think Keith is training for? *(Inferential)*

EXTENDING VOCABULARY

week	How many days are in a week? What are the names of the days? What other names do you know for periods of time?
meal	What sounds are in the word *meal*? Which letters make the long /ē/ sound?
cutie	Read the word *cutie*. Which letters make the long /ē/ sound? What is the base word of *cutie*?

MOVING BEYOND THE TEXT

1. What are some activities that you do every week?
2. What do you wish you didn't have to do each week?
3. How are your weekends different from weekdays?
4. Which activities in the book would you like to try? Why?

TIME TO WRITE

Write about your weekly routine. What do you do each week?

PRACTICE WORDS

Reed speech speeches sweet

each

week we cheek

Keith see weeds baby meal

green eats peas reads sleep

he Nelly team Lee be

leap chief beam beach scruffy

donkey Neil cutie feeds lucky